B'KLYN

poems

Richard J. Fein

Richard Fein

Dear Heidi,
Thanks for the invitation.
Best wishes,
Richard

Editor: Clarinda Harriss
Graphic design: Ace Kieffer
Front cover art: Berenice Abbott
Back cover photograph: Miriam Fein-Cole

The cover photograph, by Berenice Abbott, "Warehouse, Water, and Dock Streets" (from *Changing New York*) is used with the permission of The Museum of the City of New York.

BrickHouse Books, Inc. 2011
306 Suffolk Road
Baltimore, MD 21218

Distributor: Itasca Books, Inc.
© 2011

ISBN: 978-1-935916-00-0

Acknowledgments

Acknowledgment is made to the editors of the journals
where the following poems originally appeared:

The Deronda Review: "Dear Yiddish," "The Cold Dictionary"

The Ledge: "The Statues in the Garden"

Ploughshares: "To My Brother at His Funeral"

The Poetry Porch: "The Office" (on-line)

Yiddish: "Eeriness Erupts," "*Denkmol nokh a ferd*," "Fate"

*With gratitude to Solon Beinfeld, Clarinda Harriss, Teresa Iverson,
George Kalogeris, Marcia Karp, and Steven Sher.*

Also by Richard J. Fein

Poetry

Selected Poems of Yankev Glatshteyn (translations)
Kafka's Ear
At the Turkish Bath
To Move into the House
Ice Like Morsels
I Think of Our Lives: New and Selected Poems
Mother Tongue
Reversion
With Everything We've Got (translations)

Prose

Robert Lowell
The Dance of Leah

"for the child shall die an hundred years old"

Isaiah 65:20

For Eli, Ari, Maya, and Joshua.

Contents

I

Three Men

I

The sounds scraped on the fiddle between the apartment houses rose up to our
          kitchen window
and prompted my mother to dig up a few pennies and pack them in a square piece
          she cut from a brown paper bag.
She handed me the wrapped coins to carefully toss from our sill
so the mute packet would land intact near where the fiddler was playing,
and I heard vague strains of Eastern Europe that rose up from the alley between
          the whitewashed bricks.

II

"Kesh-kloze, kesh-kloze," he bellowed up to the windows from the alley,
and sometimes my mother gave me old clothes to bring down to him.
He held them out before him, studied them, and handed me some coins to bring
          back to her.
He rolled all the clothes he collected into a long stretch of Manila paper
(even wider and thicker than the sheet of waxy paper Mr. Berman's hand lifted and
          tore off from his brawny cylinder in the butcher shop)
then wrapped up the bundle, with a loop of hemp running through, and slung it over
          a shoulder, like a doughboy's roll,
and vanished with the old clothes he gathered from us and our neighbors,
until his voice rose up to us next time, "Kesh-kloze, kesh-kloze."

III

He wore a suit, a beard, and a yomica and came into our apartment
to take the *pushka* heavy with pennies, so stranger-Jews could plant trees in
          the Holy Land,
leaving us a new empty can with the blue palm tree on the white background and
          the blue Hebrew lettering,
and the edge lipping the top of the box, and the dark slit the tips of our fingers
          touched.
He only spoke Yiddish, and of the two of us only my mother understood, and the
          box rattling with pennies vanished into Zion.

From the Diary of Yankev Rivlin

(Feb. 26, 1934)

How strange, growing up in Lodz
or growing old here on Broome St.,
never having danced for joy—
yet last night, stamping home
after the Fred Astaire movie,
the only footprints my own,
I watched bulbs burning
under their snow-ribbed helmets
tilted rakishly from wind and wear, snow
tufting the numbered tags
on telephone poles, meringue-treated
cars deserting their models, curbs
softening to pavement, and
I could
romp in my boots anywhere.

(Dec. 10, 1947)

A few berries dangle on long stems,
catching light in their crimson wither.
Some tips of twigs darkly bud
with aborted life or forgery of spring,
though branches mostly taper at the end.
I strain to find that node of transfer
where a twig ends and alters to air
or air ends and becomes the twig,
exactly where one is endowed
with the power of turning into the other.
That point changes through the seasons
as the tips stretch and blossom, or narrow
to claws, or fall as the park attendant's
curved blade slices deeper and deeper,
the trunk left with a glaring nubble
where the branch once started out.

A Poem Without a Name

—Avrom Sutzkever

Redfooted—
death-length, you step towards me
among the moist wild strawberries,
through dark-high forests—
you approach, without expression, without a face.

A burning mirror pours from my memory.
I drink my tearpotion that you induced.
Each little drop has its own separate, solemn taste.
The fermenting pain of the residue sinks in deeper, deeper!
I drink my own tearpotion and—
am I mad or drunk?
My eye a victim of your stare,
your lip—my lip.
Good morning, face:
The little drop of blood, my kiss, behind time's shutter
is lively and my death-kin.
Each of our mouths clamped to one of her nipples—
warmth, sweet drops;
my first murder in life,
committed near a river, near the gate of Paradise.

The river later drowned itself.
A startled wave escaped and rolled
out from its confined current; it will never
be older than its sixteen years.

My speech is your muteness I cut apart into words—
conjured—and send back to its source.
But only that pulsing vein in my temple—those words you occupy—
confers my ceaseless expiring joy.

Since the words can't return to their source,
you disappear, without expression, without
a *bruder's* face. I
covet the bed of your grave.
Redfooted—

death-length, you step towards me
among the moist wild strawberries,
through dark-high forests.

(from Yiddish)

To My Brother at His Funeral

Flying over many states,
driving through many streets,
I come to the Chapel in the Pines,
where a film of your life shows our trunks
bunched in at the crotch as we take turns
burying each other in the sands of Far Rockaway,
each standing by a mound, like archaeologists
discovering tombs, tombs of their own making.

At your plot overlooking ABC and CBS,
which you wanted sprinkled with your ashes,
a green box, like the one holding my valuables,
is passed among the mourners, while a workman
jumps into the grave. Frightened by imagining
you as ash, I recall your body at the beach.
The minister announces, "David's brother will read *Kiddush*."
I correct him, and make my own mistakes.

Divided, we built a memory-bridge
out of what we saw from our bedroom window,
like two scholars of an illuminated manuscript
that is fading under their very eyes,
and they the only ones left to read it—
Vic's barbershop pole scrolling up, or scrolling down,
"Gabilla's Knishes" in Hebraicized lettering on the delivery truck,
Goozhie and Lovie, like lab partners, gauging the handicaps at
             Kramer's candy store.

The Girl at the Movies

Peek-a-boo kneecaps behind the frayed slashes of her jeans, she saunters along
> her row,
slouching just in front of me, bracing her shins against the back of the seat in front
> of her,
her convex knees pushing through the slits, her neck a touch bent.
"You know, this is one of the best," I exult to my friend—
we ex-teenage connoisseurs of the art cinemas in the Village and the grind dumps
> on 42nd St.
"The best," he pronounces.
"*Grand Illusion,* the best movie ever made?"
the girl asks, the moons of her knees swinging toward us.
"Hmm-hmm," my friend lilts.
"He's seen it twenty times," I pipe up. "I've seen it only six."
"I've never seen it before," she confesses, "though I have seen *La Règle du Jeu,*"
and, after a slight pause, thinking we don't understand, explains, "*Rules of the Game.*"
"We know it well," my friend informs her, "but it's not as good as this one."
"As a matter of fact," I clue her in, "some of the actors in *Grand Illusion* also appear
> in *Rules of the Game,*
like the guy who plays the gamekeeper, and the guy who flirts with his wife, and
> Dalio, the star of the movie, who is Rosenthal in this one."
"Later, he turns up in *Casablanca* as a croupier," my friend tacks on.
As the light dims, her boyfriend suddenly shows up to sit beside her.
We're all looking ahead now, and soon Maréchal hum-sings as he leans over the
> gramophone while its elbow-arm rides the record grooves—
"Frou-Frou. . .Frou-Frou-Frou. . .Tra la la la. . .la. . .la. . .Frou-Frou. . ."—
and the gray circular top of his black kepi comes into view,
with the closeup of its white arabesque braid, and we're taken by the weave.

After the last scene— Maréchal and Rosenthal up to their knees in snow, slogging
> their way across the border, from Germany to Switzerland—
I hope the girl will turn around and talk about the movie.
I want to know what she feels about it, having seen it for the first time,
but she quickly moves out, slipping on her coat as she goes, her grinning boyfriend
> right behind her,
her moon-knees out of sight now.
My friend and I linger, relishing moments in the movie, especially things I hadn't
> noticed before—
the late accretion of music, how tough-minded Rosenthal could be, like when it's
> time to leave Elsa, or how Boeldieu, who detests flutes, plays one
> to secure the escape.

"It all fits, it all makes sense," I get aroused, "even what looks accidental or casual."
The theater empty, we straggle out of our row, my friend still observing on the
                    move,
"How sad Rauffenstein is—a man losing his world—when he snips off the flower
                    from the potted geranium, and closes the eyes of the dead Boeldieu,"
and, as we reach the door, "that title sure grows on you."

The Patient

Lunar antlers sprout from ears,
droop, blacken, thicken, merge
into a cold zodiac roving
on my chest and back, followed
by two thumping fingers.
A chaste-white duster—
starched, creaseless, glossy,
its flat, crisp, linear pockets
like slits sealed into the cloth—
deploys, Indian file, four-eyed
buttons that light on me:
"A CATscan, EKG, carotid duplex."
A punctured neck bells out
from a clipboard and a bulbous thumb
presses on a nub, and a point scurries
across a pad I never see,
and my gurney's steered away
while I'm staring at the ceiling
panels' systematic perforations
that change to random wormy nicks,
and slabs of fitted frosted glass
that change to ice tray grids
with their neon cubes—
and I'm delivered to an alcove
where a technician jiggles my bracelet,
my name purplish, stamped and smudged,
and I hear my blood gurgling on a screen.

The Fourth Man

Last night I dreamed my last uncle died.
Abner Baron, that ardent Zionist, also died.
And Rabbi Liebowitz, who bar mitzvahed me, died,
And I fell in love with an Afro-American poet
with a pockmarked face, only a fuzz of hair on her head,
as if she had been in chemo. And we nuzzled cheeks
and cooed and murmured—Yes, we'd read poems together—
yes, she'd consider conversion—and I was amazed
I could fall in love with someone so different,
who wasn't even pretty, her cheek so warmly touching mine
as I told her about the three men who came to our neighborhood when I was
        a child—
the man who scratched sounds on his fiddle in the alley;
the man who called up to the windows for old clothes;
the man who entered our apartment and only spoke Yiddish and collected our box
        of pennies.

Her cheek could feel my cheek moving—bone and hollow
to bone and hollow—as I told her the story of the visiting men,
and she took in the story as if now it were hers too,
and then it was my cheek's turn to feel her cheek moving, telling
me about the peddler with the beard and foreign accent carrying kitchenware
and packets of notions from farm to farm in the Carolinas.

II

Spring Cleaning in Childhood

We wrestled the mattress toward the floor
and tilted it up against the high dresser,
whose curved top drawer was always locked.
Our dust rags plied the exposed coils,
the tips of our fingers bunching up
the deeper they got into the nose of those funnels.
She did her half of the coils. I did mine.
Having worked at those spirals and the networks
connecting them, we walked the bedspring up,
pushing it farther and farther,
each of us wading in between two slats,
the metal framework rearing above us. Palms
buoyant on the coils, I braced the bedspring
while she wiped the slats, adjusted
their spacing, and swept her rag along the bedstead
before sliding it across the lacquered brown headboard
from its carved finial down to the revealed edge.
I watched, standing on the floor that was under
their bed, looking at it from above, standing
there where scatter rugs didn't hide the wood,
the dark stained nailheads like eyes
scorched into the glossy planks of pine, though
even then I was only seeing the floor in parcels
and had to keep my steps within the slats.

Looking like a field hand, a red bandanna
knotted to her scalp, she said,
"OK, dear. Be careful. Let's lower the spring now."

Catskills

The clews of a hammock hanging from hooks,
my father sleeping away an afternoon
outside my grandmother's boarding house,
my aunts, uncles, cousins coming and going,
signaled by the muffled banging
of screen doors, I a bug
who knows his genus, scampering
into a crevice of his territory

Priming the Pump

(Catskills, 1940)

Calling me into the kitchen, Grandma said, *Brengkaltvaserfunpump*,
her warrant of words I couldn't untangle but understood
as she handed me the celery-green pitcher filled
with water from the sallow faucet. Outside, I tilted
the pitcher at the spout and poured into the guts of the shaft
and pumped the lax handle until I could feel it stiffen,
as if at first resisting its own effort to bring up the water;
then I heard gurglings and finally the water gushed
onto the unleveled, overlapped sheets of aluminum
fixed to the platform by nailheads shinier than buttons on a bellhop.
Water slicking the silver and spotting
my sneakers, shorts, and shirt, I kept the mouth
close to the flanged nozzle and watched how frantic
bubbles tempered to beads ringing the lip of water.
I carried the pitcher back through the screen door,
setting it down for my parents, aunts, uncles, cousins—
all of us summer boarders—
                                        and sixty-seven years later
I return to that scene, and see a third hand
of mine, whose index finger spells out my name,
in spectral clarity, within the mist covering the celery-green glass.

Karakul

His small splayed hands cruised down his aunts'
coats overlapping on the bedspread. The furs
purred and smoothed, yielding to the advances
of his descending palms, all the fur supple
except that wiry-glossy black jacket
with the deep piles, whose crevices
his fingers skidded into, this Central Asian
curl, a resistant twist his childhood
had never pictured in Mary's little lamb.
His touch rebuffed by the kinky stuff—
black knolls unobliging to his forays,
his fingering for the fluent drift—
he saw those coarse loops lustered
to a louring, palm-repellent shag.
That frizzled, defiant Tadzhik thicket
denied a buoyant glide, and though he
coaxed with pat, stroke, poke, press, rub,
wanting the coat to relent under his touch,
the nitid tangle of hairs refused to unclench,
fixed, like frozen ripples on a black lake.

Dothan

"for I heard them say, Let us go to Dothan."

Genesis 37:17

If it's distance that makes the difference, why try to bridge it?
But what if keeping distance stems from fear of turning into them?
Then again, what if your going out to meet them
is a pretense of camaraderie, a sham of itself—
the distance ineradicable even should you join them—
just as the flag you and they publicly swear allegiance to
is for them the colored concentration of loyalties
but for you a measured piece of cloth, and regional dyes
sporting pocked lozenges circumscribing an axe-moon?
And yet, in any event, hasn't it touched you too, wind-
crisp above the anthem, the field, the salute, the tribe?
And aren't you taken with your tunic, that florid tunic?
So round and round you go, asking yourself:
By keeping the distance, do you lose your life or gain it?
Will you follow the directions some stranger might give you
to their wagons, their tents, their flocks, their fires?
But not seeking them—doesn't that show loyalty to your own genesis?
Or, might better words and a better life come if you go to them,
all of you sons of the same father? Employing distance,
you reason, your not going to them, will finally be your way of having
                    gone to them,
you, strongest, by not being complicit with them,
and you conclude, "What truth do they live in that I envy?"

Then you hear yourself asking a stranger, "Tell me,
do you know where they've gone tending the sheep?"

Eeriness Erupts

—Itshe Slutski

Eeriness erupts even from my home,
and estrangement overgrows my kinship to it,
like grass on an untrodden path.
My shtetl nourished in me
a hatred of her affection,
for in her very furrows where my life was born
it also died.

The old cats, climbing the walls,
still carry a lament in their teeth like a squirming mouse:
Every day a new trembling breaks out,
like scabies on the skin of the Jews,
and uncertainty, like a fire, smolders in each house.

Hunger pangs cut
into Jewish skin
like the tearing of one's clothes
after a death.
And in famished houses of worship,
Kaddish, like *Neilah*,
is chanted
as the Gate of Judgment shuts.

(from Yiddish)

III

The Office

Where in my life of teaching was the glowing coal that might touch my lips?
I came to hope that poetry might couple my furtive and my outward lives,
that I might become capable, as pride of soul and sympathy for the world stretch
                    and balance each other,
and that I might make poems I never could before,
finding my childhood a source,
finding in my grainy truths what I need to know,
finding the words of my untenured life,
finding in supposéd retirement my real work,
like my double-take when my three-year-old grandson's fingertips tested the little
                    white hairs that have come to sprout on the ridge and slopes
                    of my nose,
my skin animating his curiosity, his puzzlement at what adults carry around
                    with them,
my body transmitting all that material of wonder to him,
just as my aunts' and uncles' did when my child-eyes studied them close-up:
red nails drumming on images of fruits imprinted into the oilcloth,
or an oval ruby in a class ring embossing a pudgy, hairy finger,
or a mouth-soaked stain garnishing the cap of a cigar, and at the stump-end leaves
                    singeing into a lacy cylinder of ash.

Blocks I walked and re-walked; blocks I peered down; blocks I spurned. . .
yet now, residing in rooms where poems lurk, murmur and near,
perhaps I can say what I have stumbled over for most of my life is a kind of
                    appointed ground,
my own lot littered with my own refuse;
I'm still crossing a corner in Brooklyn while walking the streets I'm on now,
the poems and novels I taught now speaking to me as never before, my finally taking
                    them personally,
and, now, past my middle years, the revelation of my own slowness seems to make
                    all stupidity sacred.
After all that training and application, I wonder if I entered teaching only because
                    I had to leave it finally—

finally the books becoming mine, no longer attached to degrees, no longer the
                    materials of insulation,
and I walked away from the desk at the head of the class,
divorced the nomenclature of advancement,
cast away the grades that encouraged or stifled,
left behind those young people I helped to read, and the handful, perhaps, I inspired,
abandoned explications of a line, an image, an ambiguity, a career—

released now to enter the very material I taught, premonitions of possession having
come to me before, as when,
one afternoon, the sun a slash across my desk,
I swiveled toward the tight shelves in my office, housed in an old dorm,
and crooked two fingers, steadily working out my Pound
(in the New Directions *Selected*, so deftly formatted for holding)
and read to a student the first of the *Cantos* because I wanted to show him how
poetry works on you before you understand it
and then reveals itself more and more as you read again and again, and you come to
watch the poem materialize
as when the lens of a microscope clarifies more and more and you see sperm
wriggling and dashing about,
and in my urge I delivered the lines for both of us, my voice surging over the desk
and the book, as if we, the student and I, were discovering poetry for
the first time,

But first Elpenor came, our friend Elpenor,

marveling at how we surrendered to what we knew or did not know, or had only
glimpses of, or began perceiving as we went further, or sensed in the
transformation of old sounds, or never grasped,
as we were carried away by the canto to lands of rites and darkness, prophecies
and tasks,
carried over water by the power that irascible poet brought to his words,
that overbearing man, the master of the snarl, eventually so broken and
self-betrayed, so tormented in his disjointed strolls, so deranged
with shaggy and rugose face of old age—
like an Odysseus who foundered on the rocks he himself steered towards,
an exhausted wanderer who never reached home, washed up on an obscure coast,
though once his goatee was jewelled to the drilling point, and he prompted Yeats
to shed his old green cloak—
that even a Jew might feel sorry for his pitiful spirit,
this man whose first canto summoned fellow veterans, a dead mother, a farseeing
mentor, and an old love—
the student and I sensing the powers that dwelt in my office as I read aloud from
that book, as I held that red binding in my hands, and tested its grainy
texture with my fingers.

I left teaching at 62, and poetry came to me as never before

Jew'accuse

Pound helped me translate Glatshteyn,
even taught me how to read.
Yet I would place him in hell,
where he runs around and mutters
into his diamond-point beard,
"Who have I hurt? What have I won?"
I learn from him, make a distinction
between his hate and his aesthetics.
I hear Manger, Margolin, Glatshteyn
rising and charging,
Du host undz farratn.
"You've betrayed us."

                  But I keep on circling
between them and Pound, between me
and Pound,

                subject to a distinction.

Walking Home on *Shabbes*

(for Rabbi Ben-Zion Gold)

"We lack a liturgy to mark the Holocaust,
or even an appropriate day. I prefer
Kristallnakht as the time for us to mourn,
but the politics of Israel demanded
we connect the loss of. . ."
Suddenly you stop, and I watch you
reach over a fence and break off a twig
from a shrub, crush a bunch of shoots
and bring them to your nose. "My father
showed me this when he took me to Ger
that very first time to see the *rebbe*."
Der tate hot dos mir gevizn
dos ershte mol vos mir zaynen geforn tsum Gerer.
Gently, you bring the scaly leaves to my nose
and the faint cedar smell reminds me of the chest
in which my mother summered our winter clothes.
Reaching your door, you still hold
the crushed leaves in your fingers.

A Photograph of a Yiddish Poet in the Park

The slats of air paralleling the slats of wood
slotted into the concrete flanks of the park bench
shaped and bore you as you read *Di goldene keyt* in '52
when I, a grad student, was squeezed into a subway seat
of imitation plaited straw, my nose buried in the *Kenyon Review*.
Thirty-four years later, plunged past all my training,
my teaching others how to read, I look at you, declare to you,
now gone—"For who did you write if not for me?"
As I translate you, your lines insist my throat
and tongue possess their sounds, eat and relish
their syllables and vowels and consonants I once spurned.
There's no making up for our having failed to embrace
what we should have years ago, though a missed chance
might haunt us and reshape as if it were something new.
Yankev—your first name that middle name I never used.
The first time I read you, blades and handles chinked
in the divider in the kitchen drawer as I jiggled out
a serrated steak knife and poem by poem
sliced my way through your uncut deckle-edged pages
so thriftily published in Buenos Aires, as if
your words were quickened by those pages nearly rippling
beyond their covers and conferring a furbelow on the book.
And after each slice, my fingers descended the pulpy page
blazed with your letters, carpentry-letters
spellbinding the once estranged and summoned eyes of my childhood,
letters tooled one after the other—O, those serifs,
those flexures, horizontals and verticals both thick and fine.
And now, as if that shot of you is a still that moves
 into a movie, you close your journal, look resigned,
get up from the green slats and the airy slats, to go
back somewhere, and I, up from the subway, watch you
vanish in the traffic:
                    "Go, therefore, leaving
me Yiddish, for I need to pull out, fumble around in,
and take from that crowded drawer of memories,
and re-make them and you and myself."

Dear Yiddish

(for my 75th birthday)

When you whispered into my ear,
"You must come to know me now,"
I saw I must spend my life learning you,
never mastering you, as if I must not master you
but learn again and again how to breathe your words,
how to spell out what was always inside of me
even as I turned away from you, you
now apprising, "I am what you must reconfigure."
Ikh bin vos du muzst ibershtaltikn.
For the first time I sense the lush logic
of old poems cherishing flowers and bushes
that flourish from their rootedness in old graves.
I remember how once, having reached a dead end—
the lights out, my books tiered against the walls,
my typewriter hooded, my desk become its wooden surface—
I lay on the Persian rug in my study, stretched rigid
for an hour or more, or less. I couldn't say.
I rose up, learned to shape you, to bring you
out of me, language buried within me. I attended
each letter, those bonding particles of sound,
those nuances I learned to sense within you. Closer
than we supposed, you and I lodged in each other.
Attached to your letters, your words, by hook
or by crook, I am attached to myself. Shameless,
as if every touch between you and me comprehends
all that you have been through, I explore you,
I bend over you, I reach inside of you.
Give me whatever breath you have.

Granite Wings

—Avrom Sutzkever

The cold granite wings
sunk in the earth,
bound with chains
to the body below—
the only witnesses
it is still here.

The cold granite wings
sunk in the earth
draw closer to the body below.
They start to shiver
as a sunshower
collects in their crevices.
Now they wrench
themselves loose
from the earth, from the chains,
along with the dust-green body.

The cold granite wings—
where are they flying off to?
If I knew
I would go on foot,
go with them
in my dream of them,
along with the dust-green body.

(from Yiddish)

Denkmol nokh a ferd

(Memorial for a Horse)

—Avrom Sutzkever

A horse with a red soul
and two nightingale eyes
revealed itself like an angel,
and halted, breathless, in the snow.

Let us remember the horse
before the snows melt.

Wolves could not overtake him
and glaring snowdrifts blind him
until the rider, that naked boy,
brought him from the enemy's lines.

Let us remember the horse
before the snows melt.

The rider knelt before his deliverer,
as if they were dreaming together. . .
and later shaped a memorial—
a horse shaped of snow.

Let us remember the horse
before the snows melt.

And everyone saw that wonder,
how the red soul of death
arrived under that snowy hide—
in that horse, shaped of snow.

That horse, remember that horse
before the snows melt.

(from Yiddish)

A Born-Again *Song of Myself*

All versions issued during Whitman's life and the variants huddled in the margins,
       squeezed between lines, and fleshed out to notebooks rose from their pages,
rose and visited me last night, keeping me awake, and I conceived of making the best
       version possible,
making a grand redaction out of all the possibilities he put before me,
and the born-again poem came out of me;
it broke its bag of water inside of me, and the water, filthy serums,
       blood, and strange matter ran out of me,
the baby's yawp the first sound I heard after I bore down and pressed the poem
       into being,
this the fruitfulness from reading *Song of Myself* in trolley cars, in subways, in
       classrooms, in parks, in the barracks, and on the boardwalk,
from reading it to girlfriends I could get to listen to it,
even though I admit, O Walt, of trying to use it in place of just giving myself to them,
       bare in my desires and hesitations,
yet you too knew what it meant to disguise your loves—your coded names—
and I went on reading the poem year after year, as I read the Hebrew Bible, and
       Yeats, going back and back to it,
and from my rummaging in your marginalia and crossouts and substitutions, and
       from my sifting your lines, and steadily measuring their depths,
it became the poem we gave each other, the poem we generated, the poem I
       returned to you out of all the parts and possibilities you put before me—
       our composite poem—
and we sat in Camden, taking turns reading stanzas, the poem shaped like its first
       version, launching down the pages without sections, one long poem—
       our compounded poem—
and as dusk crept over the Atlantic, over Montauk, over Brooklyn, and came to
       Mickle St.,
we read our work, taking turns, our voices antiphonal,
and we were blessed, dear Walt, altered by the augmentation of our own words in
       the penetrating dusk. . .the reading, the poem, our lives catching fire and
       passing between us.

       (December 5, 2007)

IV

Jade plant leaves
among orange-red flowers
tissued and puffed
like Chinese lanterns

jut from my head and neck
in this inner theater,
my scalp and skin seedbed
of each magnified leaf

and swollen flower.
I used to watch
women potting jade plants
in pudding stone urns

on brick porch railings
or flanked stoops. Most
of the year, cigarette butts
and crumpled gum wrappers

bred in the urns. All over
my childhood borough, vessels
with low relief of looping wreaths,
detached berries,

and crude frets at the base.
Classic Brooklyn—urns
glinting in their mealy stone
where my fingertips

found craters,
like the crevices
and gouges in bricks
or in barks of the lindens

on boulevards. Now I watch
dull-glazed leaves
and tumorous flowers
sprout from me, closeup-

vegetations of my body,
germinations of my vintage skin,
botanic distentions. But
didn't you ask last night:

How do poems grow?

Snow and Tree

The snow is subject to the tree—
to crevices between the collage
of shards of bark; to curves,
breadth, forks, and nodes
of branches; to the poking of twigs,
their degrees of thinness, their tips
diverging into further tips;
to knobs, knurs; to groined
recesses at the base of the trunk;
to abrasions on reptilian digits
tapering to roots tapering to hairs.

And the tree is subject to the snow—
to the thick or thin coating
as the snow's inclined or driven;
to the uneven sleeving of the branches
depending on how the snow clings
or contours along the sides,
the dappled run of the bark;
to the puff, or button, at the tips
of twigs, like ends of swabs, or foils;
to ice gouged in the bole's hooves,
as they taper into the ground.

Two Shrubs

Two shrubs shrouded in burlap
ghost the garden of a corner house
while an amputated tree bears witness,
blunted, bald, gleaming arms
above sawdust spattered on the ground.
Walking home from the drugstore,
I stop, getting as close as I can,
pressing in between black spears
with their gilded tips. The shrubs,
wrapped to burly abstractions,
guide the walk while the invalid tree
withdraws from the gate. I keep on
staring at those shrubs and that tree;
branches lopped to spectral stumps,
glaring particles, and stems
muzzled in dented bags
stalk me,
like the Rx'd gelcaps
planted on my sisal breakfast mat,
sedated Mexican jumping beans.

The Statues in the Garden

(after Atget)

Some of them invert and blur in lake and pool,
where water films the trees. Or wearied
by cornucopia, drapery, scutcheon and armor,
they yearn to vanish into plinth or base.
Stain, chip, crack, corrosion, fungus
are all too slow for what they desire.
Older than the myths they represent, they
are no longer fixture, ornament, sanction,
no longer the resigned guardians of stairs.
They envy the litheness of trees, the light
portioned by the veins of leaves, or the darkness
of bark, shards aboriginal to the touch.

Bacon-Bird

The rust-guts of a Bacon-bird
admit the cold spring light
while the nearby blue pansies—
turned to crocuses at second sight—
quiver and glisten in the breeze.

Akimbo-like, the dirtied wings
of the bird bracket the exposed
innards, all that certain corrosion;
neck, chest and belly beaked,
wormed and nibbled in their ruin.

I edge closer, kneel, lean, and peer
into the spoils of the bird lying
under the spread of a copper beech
with elephant skin and elephant feet.
I edge closer to the bole's blank cartouche

and nippled burls. Piecemeal,
the Bacon-bird seeps
into the ground while geese
waddle around, soil the lawn,
or dawdle under the trees.

The Bacon-bird changes to leaves.

(Mt. Auburn Cemetery, 2008)

The Pond

(at Mt. Auburn Cemetery)

The diminished pond scummed over years ago,
and every time I walk down Dell Path
I see the widening muddy margin between the dim shine
and the raised rim where I stand and think of as the shore.
I always marvel, as I take my descent,
how the 19th century indented those vaults
into the slant of the hill and tilted in the coffins
without them and their bodies plunging down into the pond,
and how the gravediggers tiered crosses and gravestones, and embedded slabs,
turning the whole place into an amphitheater, death, *in situ*,
without corpse and stone being carried away by erosion, tumble, or cave-in.
Splayed leaves are pasted on the green coating of the pond as if
nature learned from a children's art class how to stencil itself.
When I'm here at the bottom I always stare
for a few respectful minutes at the olive-green counterpane,
before I hunt around for a stone. . .of the right heft,
edge up as close to the mud as I can, brace
my feet near the edge, limber up my arm,
aim for the center, and pitch my stone into the pond.
After the plop and sudden opening to water,
I feel a kind of childhood joy at having tampered
with the solemnity of the mantle. The green film
inevitably recovers from the shock and closes in again,
like the narrowing shutter at the end of an old movie.
As much as I'm fond of breaking up that stagnant green
and exposing the eye of the water for a short time,
it's the closing up again I find, to my habitual surprise,
I've come to look forward to, and to harbor,
as if the real reason I throw in the stone is that I'm taken again
and again to testing the pond. My life, beyond the
stratagems of my sure-footed stances supporting my pitch,
impels me to trouble that algae and watch it occlude again,
oblivion covering the stone as the opening slowly shrinks,
this game of toss-and-stare I came upon as a child.

V

At the Automat

The crone-cashier perched on her stool
as her pimpled rubber thimbles flicked
at the hoard of nickels and poked our change
toward the marble trough, where I combed it
into my cupped palm, my other fingers
free to count out the requisite coins.
After feeding the slots to their satisfaction,
turning knobs and levers—the little doors opening,
the brass faucets releasing their hot flow—
we carried our mugs of coffee and slices of pie
to a waiting table, where a friend of mine
suddenly materialized, seated there with us,
and you became cold, saying something like,
"Once again you've brought someone to judge me."
Adamant, you rose and ran to the subway. I detoured
to slip our trays onto the pile, and ran after you,
almost tumbling down the subway steps, barely
keeping my balance by skidding along the handrail.
You were nowhere to be found. I paid my fare,
and just as I tensed before pushing against the turnstile,
its heavy wooden arm like a bone clubbed at the end,
I saw my Indian nickel staring back at me,
magnified in a window of light below the coin slot—
the buffalo with its brooding hump, a satyr's tickler-beard.

My Own Private Eye

(after Sextus Propertius)

My own private eye, I hid in a doorway across the street
from Cynthia's place. She had called me in the morning,
"Don't show up 'til seven," but I got there early to get the goods
on her, and sure enough, she showed up with a guy,
quickly sent him on his way, then went inside,
but came out quickly, to check if he rounded the corner.
She spotted me, motioned me forward with her arm
as if she were directing traffic, then faced her door, holding the knob,
waiting for me to cross over and catch up to her.
Without saying a word, we went inside, heard our trudge
on the marble stairs, worn down in the middle like steps to a shrine.
Once inside, as she stood by the bed, her arms wormed
out of their coat, and her feet kicked off their shoes: "So,
you're spying on me. Don't trust me, huh?
See, my lipstick isn't smeared.
Is my skirt crooked, my sweater mussed?
See, my bun's tight, needled at the knot.
I'm perfectly calm. You're the one who's breathing hard.
Do you want to check my handbag for my diaphragm and cream?"

I had no words, my tongue trolling my dry mouth.
I reached out to touch her—her black eyes darker than ever,
her blond hair lighter—but the back of a hand flicked me away,
and as she turned and steamed off to the bathroom,
the seams of the stockings charged up from the calves
to the lower thighs, and slightly curved
until they disappeared under the skirt.
Again and again,

>   I regret my stupid watch,
>   see her spotting me,
>   her arm crooked at her head,
>   motioning me from my hiding place

her whole arm

Amtrak

"We're not getting anywhere.
All you do is keep on asking
why, why. I've told you again
and again, I wasn't thinking.
What more do you want me to say?
You've got to put it behind you. Look
. . .huh?. . .hmmm. . .uh-huh. . .OKbye."
Sidling out, turning, as if needing
the rest room, I pause
ever so slightly, feign
at righting my balance before
going down the aisle,
shoot my furtive look at the body of the voice
on the cell phone—maybe twenty,
pale, white sweater, white skirt, running shoes,
and staring into the back of my seat
as if her eyes were burning a hole
right through the upholstery
to my antimacassar,
but what I can't keep
from fixing on
is the slab
of elliptic buttons on her lap.

The Cold Dictionary

I think again of the fix we were in,
and that fitting image comes back to me
though I never remember
which the mortise and which the tenon
(akin to my problem
with mortar and pestle)
and look up again
mortise joint,
diagrammed in my dictionary,
the segmented extension of the tenon
delineating which piece slots into which.
For the first time, I see
mortling follows,
and I think,
raveled by wrongs and rights,
how much I wove out of who we were;
and then, as if the page's
third column conspires,
mortmain follows,
like the hand that lay on us;
but this alphabet
and my obsession and play
don't solve my question:
which is worse,
not asking for forgiveness,
or being unable to give it?
Then that image comes back
and for a spell
my mnemonics works—
ah yes, ten*on* fits *in* the mortise.

But even as my unabridged,
or my sound-device,
couples term and image—
the technic of insert and reception—
I'm driven to still another question:
what makes things too late,
and we're locked into place?

Outside the Gate

She ate two down to the core
yesterday. Then getting up today
plucked one to thrust at him.

He saw she eyed the tree, hungry
from the start, yet he turned
away, afraid to say anything.

Deep into theory, his passions
civic before they were private, he
aroused her with his body of ideas.

She broke the membrane of his life.
They moved to their delights, to touch,
and then exposed their thoughts.

He stopped wanting his ideal
grounds, reached, and took a bite.
Only then were they named.

And then he came to face
what he couldn't have faced
by staying in the garden.

How could he blame her? All along
he knew she plucked the fruit
and would offer it to him.

Yet he had never said a word,
as if waiting for the day when
they gnawed, chewed, and swallowed.

Keturah

"Abraham took another wife, whose name was Keturah."
Genesis 25:1

Watching you raising your legs while bracing your back on the rug,
watching your arms at right angles, your palms facing upward,
watching each of our sons taking his turn, righting his soles in your
        stirrup-hands,
watching him stretching his arms, his hands clasping your soles,
watching you lifting him in that balancing act between you,
watching him conversely arcing over your body and trusting your powers,
I think—how different the marriage we have made,
having married for our own sake,
having had children for their own sake,
having watched them grow for their own sake.
I have looked into that book of beginnings you leave open,
so many chapters devoted to you, while I'm given only one line,
and, as I figure it, Abe, we're the first ones in the tribe
who just bathe and admire themselves, as if dealers of spice.
We have sex because we love each other.
With me, you're restored, to espouse life with evenings at home,
and I don't have to wave from the dais, or shepherd the children
at your swearing-in, or serve up smiles to the foreign dignitaries,
though I can't figure out what you write in that black notebook of yours—
waking up in the middle of the night, fingers scurrying for a pen,
before diving back under the covers, nestling up to me again,
belly to belly, or belly to back, and later back to back,
my body so attuned to your body that even while sleeping it's
watching you tossing and turning, before the day slants through the blinds.

For Us Two

(after Whitman)

Forgetting, remembering, a man and a woman exchanging
old and new memories, continued to the last, revising.

Fate

—Rokhl Korn

Can you imagine—fate speaking through the very first word,
can you imagine—fate suddenly clear in the very first look,
and you deriving from it an age-old spell,
at one and the same time your punishment, your misfortune, your happiness?

It is the smile so helpless and childishly embarrassed,
already conquered by everything now bound to come,
that your hands tremble, because at that very instant
they hold within them your whole life.

Now I know there was a reason that death passed me by,
that every stone along the way became a pillow for me,
and every border a fusion that led to you—
every fusion a far-away, unknown shore.

And even if I had been cut down before my time,
I would have had to return to myself after my death,
to carry out the fate that flowed in my blood,
to exhaust the full bitterness of my last happiness.

(from Yiddish)

Not a maw enhanced its diet. . .

Not a maw enhanced its diet,
not a snout moused novel terrains,
not a syrinx cruised the gamut,
not a paw sublet its haunts,
not a pinion banked a flight,
because of what he named
each creature. But when she came,
he murmured her name—their lives
whetted, animated.

Genesis 1-3

In your lingering anger you must concede all that you gained from me—
once again taking books personally, the way you read them in childhood,
in adolescence, and as a young man on furlough from drills, fatigues,
       and barracks.
No longer class assignments, they reveal themselves and enter you, release you
       on your own cognizance,
you, like me, just as subject to the climes of history, to the waiting rooms,
       coaches, and inns inhabited by a character in a novel—
why should I be different, a breed apart from those heroines, suffragettes
       of desire,
or why you any different from those young men fresh from the provinces who
       blunder into themselves?
With me you will eat new fruits, navigate and trade beyond cabotage,
speak pidgins or sign or practice conjugations you thought you'd never want
       to know.
Some necessity drives me to expel you from your wish for exemption,
and to test if you could forgive me in our process,
as if we chose each other so we might be better than who we were.
I am threefold—a memory, a presence, a presiding force.
And now songs speak to you as never before, not only the cleverest and
       the saddest, but also the most sentimental;
singers and listeners, even clarinets and saxophones, even penny whistles,
knowing more than you did since they move up and down the scale,
or slide, or counterpoise their registers, or shift, or riff.
And now we take our bearings beyond the sentry's booth, rivers streaming off,
       their stone beds under a green flow,
behind us agitated red lights, and slashes of black and yellow along the lowered
       arm of a gate,
preventing us from going back, forcing us elsewhere.
You envy any unworried dog shambling along in its fur and colors, in its ribs
       under twitching flanks, making its way
with its carpentry of leg bones, its resilient foot pads—
now, come with me. We must leave. We have to go.

Some Like It Hot

Squeezing in lunch while chitchatting near the mailboxes,
bait of cole slaw dangling from your lips,
you thrust your Reuben at me—"Here, take a bite,"
the lipsticked indent of your crust and dough so close
I can see the layered moisture of the half you hold,
like the cross section of a specimen prepared for a bio class.
You come on; I pull back. But you push the meats and greens closer until
      I chomp,
my mouth filled with the remnants of grinding as I lick
my lips and delicately pincer my handkerchief out of my pocket
to make sure nothing drips on my jacket and tie.
You laugh and pick up eating where I leave off,
before you and your rosy pantsuit return to your office,
where schedules, letters, reports, and studies interbreed on your desk.
You are the ablest head we've ever had, valuing and positioning
each member of the department according to what he or she does best,
you, who know how to smooth slights, manage cleavage, make a case for a raise,
you, so bright and well read that Howe said, "she
was my best graduate student," you the star
of his CUNY seminar on Bathsheba, Tess, and *The Dynasts*.
"If scholarships hadn't carried me away from Appalachia,"
you confided to those close to you, "I'd have ended up
turning tricks in box cars, or in the cathouses of Wheeling."

Plump, sallow, blonder in bed, neck scalloped
by the flaccid collar of the flannel nightgown, wrists
in ruffled cuffs, breasts under the run of the ruche-flap
hiding the strip of blue buttons, a mussed V at the throat,
you rouse up in energetic lassitude, brace yourself
to angle up the pillow, pat a space, and I sit
on the edge of the bed as if making a house call
to hear your heart and feel your pulse and press
and thump your front and back. "How your poems going?"
you ask at each visit. "Obsessions still paying off?"
You believe in me. Your own collection will be posthumous.
Then your quivering joke, "If you climb in while I'm fibrillating
I'll whisper, 'I'm dying, Richard, dying.' "

I miss your calls, your voice so close your breath could vent through
      the perforations of my receiver.

Assisted Living

"The tragedy of sexual intercourse is the perpetual virginity of the soul. . ."

Here at Fairmount Manor,
we'll come upon each other again.
After fifty-six years,
he's back inside of me, though
my pussy needs a lot of jelly,
his dick a device
to jack it up. Despite
a thin membrane
and quick shrinkage,
we devise joy,
cooking things up,
eating together, talking,
as if for the first time,
and taking walks
around the reservoir, hoping,
even in aging,
we'll surmount Yeats's verdict,
which I copied onto the flyleaf
of *A Little Treasury of Modern Poetry,*
you remember, the book
with the red ribbon sewn in,
bound in grainy blue,
required for the course
we took last spring,
fifty-six years ago.

Old Man Greenbaum

"Whitman's passions had been public before they were private. . ."
Paul Zweig, *Walt Whitman: The Making of the Poet*

Heavy, dull summer afternoons, with nothing to do, no friends to see, or girls
        I might look up,
I'd visit the light-filled, empty loft above the stores to see Old Man Greenbaum,
a bent, rheumy man with a hooked nose and a snarling temper,
two veiny cords protruding down his neck, marking the edges of a gulley,
at its lower end a lump jolting just under the skin as he talked.
He was caretaker of the clubhouse of the East Flatbush Republican Party
(if one can believe there were any members in solid-Roosevelt Brooklyn),
and he always let me into that hall with the empty dais and the rows
of black-framed pictures of Republican presidents from Lincoln to Hoover,
and then faces of men I couldn't recognize, Protestant visages
chaste and forbidding in their well-scrubbed probity,
their necks braced in high wing collars even then on the way out.
I visited during long days, when only Old Man Greenbaum and I
walked on that floor under the stamped tin ceiling, its recurrent coffers
and bead-florals running the length of the loft, he and I alone in the
        unpartitioned light.
A cantankerous caretaker, he screeched his complaints to me,
the perfect listener, the kid who wasn't going to tell anyone,
and I weighed the distance between his moist eyes, gouged neck, pink-white
        scalp with orphan-strands, dingy jowls,
and the banners of the clubhouse he looked after night and day. Why were
        his eyes
so red he always looked like he'd been crying? Was his life only insults
heaped upon him—the cramped sleeping quarters, the tiny burner, the lousy pay?
If I could paint, like Kitaj, or Bacon, or Freud, I would capture
Old Man Greenbaum's face, his whole head, as it appeared to me back then—
the parrot-nose, the flesh that had no backing, the eyes drowned in their serum,
        the protuberant withes of the neck, its apple bulge as threatening
        as a goiter—
and in the background scumble some black-framed eminence, some
        indistinguishable
face of rectitude. I would concentrate on Old Man Greenbaum's face
the way Rembrandt caught his own face as he grew older. I want to be loyal to
        Old Man Greenbaum
who once so puzzled and frightened me—just as Whitman, moving below his
        "perfect health," shared a bed with his feeble-minded brother,
was loyal to the war wounds of another brother, to the pitiful grammar and

worries of his mother,
just as he found a way to be loyal to the young man he was, who rode with
                    the ferryhands,
who sat with the teamsters on the horse-drawn trolleys, who spent nights
in the vault of the cellar tavern, Pfaff's, the feet of the living walking above him
(how attractive and strange "the myriad feet of Broadway" above those gathered
                    below)
and contradictory loyalties found their accretions in his lines.
And in my remembering Old Man Greenbaum's face I become
a second Richard, slowly learning that true work can only surface when we face
                    what we don't want to see,
I, the withdrawn, superior socialist with fantasies of camaraderie,
leaving the safety of my opinions for the clutch of my fears.
I want to be loyal to Old Man Greenbaum's face—the Adam's apple, the cords
                    in the neck, the bloodshot eyes with their watery whites, the guttered
                    forehead, the grizzly cheeks, the blotchy scalp, the wisps of hair
                    in the ears, the bristles sprouting from nostrils—
loyal to his face, and his head, especially now, when I am as old as Old Man
                    Greenbaum was, that unkempt
complaining man who let me enter and walk around the vast loft—
his croaky voice frothing under the beaded florals of the tin ceiling—
"Dewey, you know, Dewey, he was up here a few nights ago, didn't even
                    look at me"—
and in recalling him I see myself standing in that garner of light
as if I can, after all these years, look into his eyes again—
those tarnished eyes of Old Man Greenbaum, their blood vessels like snippets
                    of thread—
wondering again, as his lantern-nose nears my eyes, if he is a blind man who
                    sees into me.

Second Childhood

The world is born again
to the potent lack of purpose—
tools abstracted to their shapes,
fabrics converted to their fibers,
metals abandoned to their glints—
and reversion engenders invention.
An old man's figurations regress to the time
he was a child and at a loss to master
what he saw except to sense those shapes
delivering him up to the residual
intimacies of things—the implacable
brick wall absorbing light, or the tires'
paralleling cuneiforms that go deeper
than the rubber they're grooved into,
all that function and fungibility
funding the commerce of sense impressions—
as if each external guise existed only to seek
the tally of itself in the child's mind.
Once, four years old, he stood in his sunsuit,
transfixed by the black-accordion neck of the Kodak,
and now, suddenly, it's the child,
with seasoned eyes, who looks at himself
succumbing to the maroon tint in the snapshot,
and feels the shoulder straps
buttoned at the chest of his sunsuit
harness his wonder.

VI

Sleep-Chasings

"I stay awhile away O night, but I return to you again and love you;
Why should I be afraid to trust myself to you?"

Whitman, "The Sleepers"

Poet, Ancient of Days—flying through the night sky where star-clusters
                    are swirling above the fields—
the tip of your beard, wind-driven, gusting back towards your cheek,
                    wedge of white hair fulgent in the night, pliant cuneiform,
a notch. . .a letter. . .a word. . .a language. . .
hairy guidon flaring out from your skin. . .
O standard I stare at, signaling me. . .longing to follow,
longing to find a clue in your body. . .
And then another closeup, your face reverting to the bristle hairs
disguising you on the frontispiece in '55. (O late young man
with your gamy nonchalance, your hip of dalliance, your hint of undershirt,
                    your first edition.)
Come back with me now through all you wrote, to stirrings, early drafts, lines
                    finding themselves, rhythms rising from delvings, first set of proofs,
taking me with you now, flying under your powers,
taking you with me now, flying under my powers,
I returning to you, you to me,
in this night, testing this night, trying to trust this night,
no escaping this night. . .or escaping you. . .
entering and re-entering other lives,
as my old age re-enters itself out of what came before

"the midnight widow"

Crouching and sprouting his hairs, the humped
back of her hand motoring the swelling finger
crooking into her, flexing deeper and deeper, her
shifting head reconfiguring fathoms of the pillow,
eavesdropping on her contrary quavers, her knowing-
she-is-dreaming infused in the dreaming, and a line
surfaces from a poem learned by heart in childhood—
"like a woman picking through straw for the egg below"—
ache, writhe, tension, release spawned by the finger

and urgent hand and wrist, her armed accomplice;
goaded into becoming a spectacle, she leers at herself
as if fevered in a mirror, each motion coupling with itself,
and watches her body knuckling under, and a sound like
deliquescence, deliquescence descends. . .seeping into her

"the head of the moneymaker
that plotted all day sleeps"

Stalled in the dark current, whose
quivering seam creeps up the BMW
engulfed in the street. . .handles
and doors locked in by the rising tide. . .
Friedman, Hayek, and Rand propped up
in the back seat. . .a broker at the wheel. . .
lines, arrows, T-cornered parking spots,
yellowed curbs, and glowing hashmarks
of the crosswalks shimmer like marine life. . .
three blind eyes dangle from black wires

*

Mannequins rigged for a crash,
Friedman, Hayek, and Rand stare ahead,
buckled in;
penned in a glass lookout,
safety engineers
with labcoats varnished
to a futuristic forensics
nestle a clipboard at a breast,
each clamp cresting
to a hole in its neck

> "Cache and cache again deep in the ground
> and sea, and where it is neither
> ground or sea."

The massing, the satin neck, the curving, the foam
topping itself, the rush, the shatter, the backwash, the gleam of the littoral
quickly fading as if a hand had peeled away the sheen,
leaving the sand merely wet, darker, sunk into the weight of itself,
until the next breaker hits, and the backwash again leaves the gleam
vanishing to a soggy firmness—over and over the bestowal
and loss of the glow until the tide goes out further and further
and the once damp sand now dries its way back to the rest of the beach—
and I go out further to stand at the newly revealed edge, where my lowest
leg hairs quiver in the water scurrying to reach me, yet sometimes failing
        to reach me—
and now your appearance, steering the horses—oh, skillful teamster—
so soon after having endured the passage, so soon after your brogue
pitched into the clutter and hue—hawkers, hustlers, hucksters—
your badged cap commandeering the clatter of horses and trolley on
        Broadway—
stopping for riders climbing aboard, for riders getting off—
the black reins looping between your hands and the bridle
as we ride uptown and downtown, from and back to the carbarn—
I watching you as you shrewdly maneuver, working up speed or slowing down—
you, oh Pete, visiting me in Camden, in my room, the hook
back of the door, the tilt of your off-duty derby,
the same you wore as we strolled the beach at Coney Island—
we together at the wet slope of Brooklyn, exactly where the fringe
of my borough expanded or contracted as the tides compelled—
how deep and large now the tracks we made as we walked along the ocean—
the delicate ridgelets where the heels begin, the clear relief
of lozenges stamped by the soles. . .the blank imprints, the varied dents
        of the rims,
depending on posture, or pace, or slant of the strand, or texture of the grains,
or the catching up, or the lagging behind, or the striding ahead—
and the even deeper indents we made where we paused, receptors of the ocean,
        starers at the offing—
how those tracks loom now, those oval molds our boots made in the moist sand,
        how we fix on each other

Orange, the frame of my new used bike glistens
as if I had just now finished the second coat,
Corsair cursive across the oval silver medallion
dowelled to the tube housing the neck of the handlebars
locked into place by nut and bolt, themselves crusted in
by grit, corroded threads, layers of paint with tiny blisters,
while abrasive rashes erupt on the tarnished chrome.
Wrench, wrist, and muscle will have to work that neck
loose and wrestle up the handlebars to a new tilt,
angling them just right, holding and fixing them into place.
Radius-spokes invent geometries between the hub
and the rim, with its dainty cap turned tight on the nipple,
each grooved to fit the other and hold in the air—all
waiting while the back wheel hovers within the kickstand—all
ready to be part of the rolling to the edges of the borough,
where sidewalks, streets, and houses give out to marshlands.

Lessons back and forth in front of the four-family houses—until
the invisible guiding hand of Iris calculatingly removes itself
from the back of the seat sporting a clip-on pouch fringed
frontier style, while I work at speed, steering, balance and hear
her shout, "Go. . .go. . ."

Not only linked letters buying bread, butter, bananas—
speech incarnate in the edibles—
but word-porcupines sprouting quills,
or breeds of sentences that stumble into their own thickets of particles,
and every errand compelled by my mother or myself
became the-way-to-the-store stratagems—
syllables verged on blockage gauging when to rush; and when to slow down,
elisions, omissions, pauses, cunning cadences, guileful emphases,
the mobilized articles, the sutures of conjunctions, the motile prepositions,

the hinges of intonations,
the maneuverings of word order, the roundaboutness, the plethoras—
each store a test, a trick, a shame, a sham, a deceit, an exposure—
the gauntlet of consonants in the purchase, the stumbling soundforsound—
world apart from FDR, Churchill, Red Barber, Stan Glatik,
from Franco, Hitler, and Mussolini—never at a loss for words,
their microphones little wheels with spokes
or perforated, shining silver lozenges, crested by call letters,
while I am delivered to the healers who cannot cure,
but cure myself when I sing, or act, or play on the street.
"Go to the store and get. . . ," and I am sentenced
to artifice, rehearsal, hocus-pocus, scheming before my turn at the counter. . .
the self-sufficient speech of manhood and middle age finally arriving,
       for a spell,
followed eventually by that throwback stuck-stuck of childhood,
like the return of polio, or finding some long-used medicine
       no longer works.

Once upon a time butter *went smoothly, and Sylvia, the grocer's daughter,*
Sylvia—with black hair and the same name as in that song
Mr. Miranda taught us in music class— Sylvia sliced in,
and with the wide blade of the golden dowelled knife Sylvia
carved out a pound from the barrel tilted in the dairy case,
and I watched Sylvia's fingers wrapping the piece in wax paper,
smoothing out wrinkles, tightening the lapover, tucking in the corners,
Sylvia's hands leaving the lump of bullion on the marble counter

                         "I turn but do not extricate myself"

Tuesday-night répeats at the old house,
lugging garbage and blue bins
of recyclables—how devoted
they wait at the skirt of the driveway;
or I re-up—both 18 and middle age, old age—
firing range, guard duty, forced march,
and Captain Scott kills himself
with the pistol from his holster;
or the Polish gang still chases me
because they eye my orange bike—

"hey kike, hey kike"—and I make it back
to the vestibule of my father's store.

The tower rose block by block,
letter by letter, on my bedroom floor,
and my little hand knocked it down
and built it again, again,

                    and again

                        "My truant lover has come and
                                 it is dark."

She watches me from the bottom of the long narrow steps leading to a
            museum, or courthouse, or library, or bureau—
I am wearing my Salvation Army tweed jacket and a handmade Irish cap
            picked up at a closeout
as I flit down those steps thin as a fire escape, attentive to the hazards of
            my quickening pace.
Our timing is perfect, both of us having just arrived, each of us older.
Wrinkled, a touch stooped, she is recovering from a long trip, and perhaps
            spent from old liaisons.
I kiss her, reassure her that that something between us is well now.
She says, "Watching you come down those temple steps, speeding up
            your descent,
leaving that epigraph-building for the wide sidewalk there below,
            breathing toward me,
I knew you want me again. Write. Especially since it's getting dark"

                        "Be careful, darkness. . .already, what
                             was it touched me?"

The lovers in the car drove onto the pier and off the pier
and the husband reading at home must now attend to the rites.
The coffins slide in, smoke rises, wind picks up, and carrying

a deposit box he walks alone on the wide roadway between the lawns
of graves and stones, toward the gate, toward the traffic.
Neither the book he turned over as the telephone rang
nor the one he was making line by line serves him now.
Evasion and yearning for a life exempted from life and for ideas
        exempted from disproof
kept him going until he found there was a curtain he had to draw back
to see the screen showing so many acts, so many shadows, so many skins,
though he did not know his words yet, his part, his cues, his motions.
And he remembers now the head of Maréchal bent over the gramophone,
listening to the song of the chanteuse as the bulgy silver arm kept the needle
        to the grooves,
and the arabesque braid on the round top of the kepi
filled the screen with woven shapes he couldn't decipher but absorbed
        with the enamored eyes of the moviegoer
(that woven braid akin to the deep crease of the fedora; the studs on the tux;
        the checkered tablecloth in the bistro—
primordial invitations to the child sitting at the movies),
and he remembers how, wounded on a reconnaissance flight, Maréchal's
        captured and lives with his fellow-POWs

                "Confused. . . .a pastreading. . . .another,
                        but with darkness yet."

Light stains the blinds, an old man's muddled elation on waking to
        unknown time
fades as "nap" sinks in to tell him it is not morning
but late afternoon and the great TASKS between now and evening lodge
        in him again,
though he stays still and re-visits those sensuous intentions
that take over on the street, or in a store, or in a living room.
He lies there amused, perplexed, happily berating himself,
"Why haven't I cooled off by now? One of the old Greeks said he had."
If once, desire was a forest where he was lost, a path off a path,
now it is what he sees but sees through a looking glass,
"to be mocked by myself and perhaps by others as well."
He doesn't budge, still under the blanket, a late afternoon luxuriousness,
and thinks of the young woman last night, in a room of young women,
who said she is learning languages but is unsure of what to do with them,
"maybe comparative literature," as her voice tested its own waters

and her neck frisked, her long hair a throwback to his fancies.
The inwardness of her eyes, the way her breasts sloped back towards her
as her hand propped her face above the litter on the coffee table,
her pauses between her sentences, her skin subjected to her bones—all
        lavishing that tentative cast about her.
"I understand her"—a thought last night he still entertains—
she, a version of himself once, and some chance he had fumbled

                              "Double yourself and receive me darkness"

In this night, testing this night, trying to trust this night,
crooking into her, flexing deeper and deeper—
marine life   gleam of the littoral   geometries between hub and rim
golden dowelled knife   skirt of the driveway   tower of blocks
long narrow steps   arabesque braid—
shapes he couldn't decipher. . .yet absorbed. . .
night source
                breathing on the day

"Eeriness Erupts": *Neilah* – The last prayer of the Yom Kippur service. The prayer is seen as marking the closing of the gates of divine judgment on the Day of Atonement.

"The Office": The third line echoes Whitman's preface to the first edition of *Leaves of Grass*. Line 22 is almost an exact quote from Henry James's "The Middle Years."

"A Photograph of a Yiddish Poet in the Park": *Di goldene keyt (The Golden Chain)*, Yiddish literary journal

"The Statues in the Garden": Some of the phrasings stem from *Atget's Gardens*, by William Howard Adams.

"Genesis 1–3": Line 13, "I am threefold. . .," reworks a sentence by Alastair Macaulay, dance critic of the *New York Times.*

"Assisted Living": The epigraph is from *Letters on Poetry from W. B. Yeats to Dorothy Wellesley.*

"Old Man Greenbaum": Thomas E. Dewey (1902–1971), elected district attorney of New York county in 1937, later became governor of New York state, and Republican candidate for President in 1948.

"Sleep-Chasings":

"the midnight widow" – "like a woman picking through straw for the egg below" is from Moyshe-Leyb Halpern's "In Central Park." The original, and translation by John Hollander, are found in *The Penguin Book of Modern Yiddish Verse*, edited by Irving Howe, Ruth Wisse, and Khone Shmeruk.

"the head of the moneymaker. . ." – Milton Friedman, Friedrich von Hayek (economists), and Ayn Rand (novelist) were prominent proponents of capitalism.

"Be careful, darkness. . ." – The movies from which images are borrowed at the beginning and end of the section are, respectively, *Jules et Jim* and *Grand Illusion.*